There are little
pigs and big pigs, pigs
with long snouts and pigs
with short snouts, pigs with
ears that stick up and pigs
with ears that flop down.
But all pigs are
beautiful.

Text copyright © 1993 by Dick King-Smith
Illustrations copyright © 1993 by Anita Jeram

All rights reserved.

First U.S. edition 1993
Published in Great Britain in 1993 by Walker Books Ltd., London.

Library of Congress Cataloging-in-Publication Data:

King-Smith, Dick.
All pigs are beautiful / Dick King-Smith : illustrated by Anita Jeram.—1st U.S. ed.
"First published in Great Britain in 1993 by Walker Books Ltd., London"—T.p. verso.
Summary: An introduction, in brief text and illustrations, to the characteristics and habits of pigs.
1. Swine—Juvenile literature. 2. Swine—Anecdotes—Juvenile literature.
[1. Pigs.] I. Jeram, Anita, ill. II. Title. III. Series
SF395.5.K56 1993
636.4—dc20   92-53136
ISBN 1-56402-148-3

10 9 8 7 6 5 4 3 2 1

Printed in Hong Kong

The pictures in this book were done in pen and ink and watercolor.

Candlewick Press
2067 Massachusetts Avenue
Cambridge, Massachusetts 02140

ALL PIGS ARE BEAUTIFUL

by
DICK KING-SMITH

illustrated by
ANITA JERAM

CANDLEWICK PRESS
CAMBRIDGE, MASSACHUSETTS

I love pigs.

I don't care if they're little pigs
or big pigs, with long snouts or short
snouts, with ears that stick up or ears
that flop down. I don't mind if they're black

or white or ginger
or spotted.

I just love pigs.

If you really twisted my arm and said, "You have to have a favorite kind of pig. What is it?" then I might have to say, "A black-and-white spotted, medium-snouted, flop-eared pig that comes from Gloucestershire"...though of all the pigs I have ever owned, my one particular favorite was a boar called Monty, who was a large white.

A male breeding pig is called a boar.

The luckiest pigs, like Monty, live outside.

Monty never looked very white, because he lived out in the woods where there was a pond in which he liked to wallow—but he looked very large. And he was.

A good coating of mud protects a pig from sunburn.

I bought him as a youngster,

but when he was full-grown he weighed

six hundred pounds. Monty was so gentle.

When I went out to feed him and his ten wives,

he would come galloping through the trees at my

call, a really monstrous and frightening sight

to anyone who didn't know what

a pushover he was.

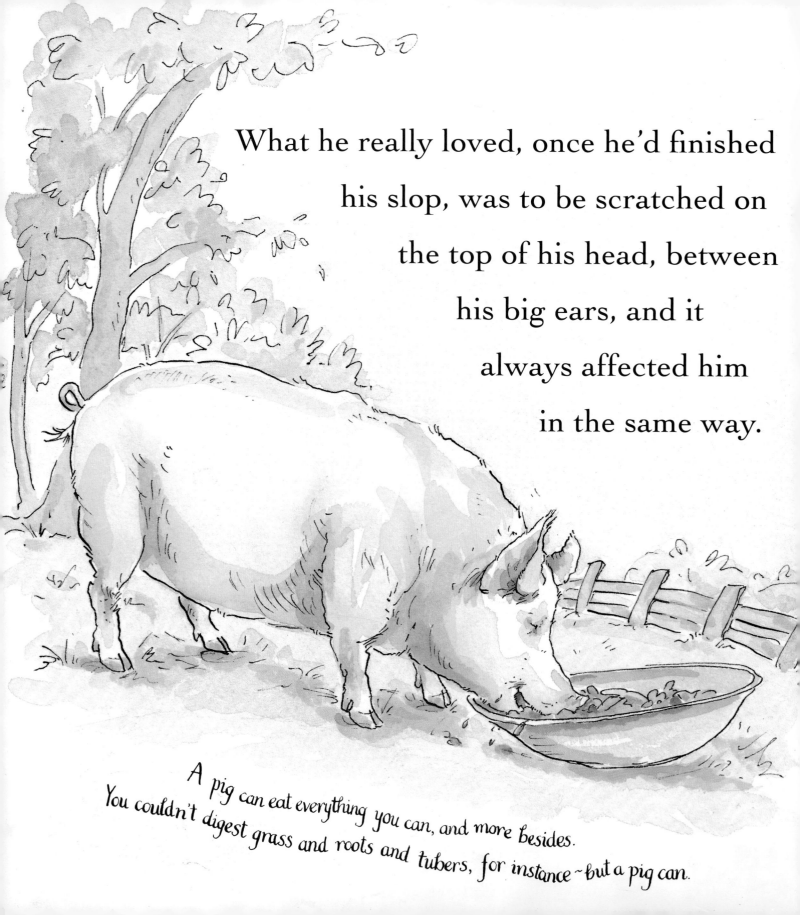

What he really loved, once he'd finished his slop, was to be scratched on the top of his head, between his big ears, and it always affected him in the same way.

A pig can eat everything you can, and more besides. You couldn't digest grass and roots and tubers, for instance ~ but a pig can.

His eyes, with their long, pale lashes,
would close in ecstasy, and slowly
his hindquarters would sink down
until he was sitting on his
bottom like a huge dog.
Oh, this is lovely,
you could almost
hear him thinking.
What more can
life offer?

Most pigs aren't so fussy. Just having their backs scratched is enough for them — they squirm with pleasure.

And of course you have to talk to them.

Pigs, like people, enjoy a good talk, so don't just stand there saying nothing.

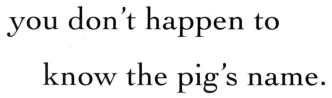

"Piggy-piggy-piggy" will do if you don't happen to know the pig's name.

Pigs have a very keen sense of smell. They can smell food even when it's buried underground.

If I'm talking to
a big fat sow
and don't
know what she's

Sows who live outdoors build large nests of grass, sticks, and bracken in which to have their babies.

called, I usually call her
"Mother" or "Mommy." They like that.

A sow normally has between eight and twelve piglets at a time.
Each piglet chooses its own private teat and returns to it for every feeding.

Sows spend their lives having babies, lots of them, and they take as good care of them as your mom does of you. Well, almost. Trouble is, newborn piglets are so small that sometimes the sow lies down and squashes one. Your mother would never do that to you—I hope!

Of course while you're busy talking to pigs, telling
them how wonderful they or their babies are,
the pigs are talking back.

Those who don't know much about them just hear grunts and squeaks, but there are all kinds of things a pig might be saying to you if you understood the language, such as:

Young female pigs are called gilts.

As you can see, pigs have cloven hoofs. They walk on their third and fourth toes.

"How kind of you to admire my children," or

"Scratch a little harder, please
—up a little, a little
to the left,
down a little. Yes,
that's it!" or

'Well, no, actually you're not
the first person to
call me beautiful," or

"This food is really excellent, yum, yum.

Thanks a lot."

But of course pigs, like people,
aren't always sunny and good-tempered,
and you might hear:

"Hurry up, you stupid
two-legged creature.
I'm starving and you're late!" or

"Don't you dare pick up
one of my babies or
I'll bite you!"
(And do be careful
—pigs have a horrible bite
so don't take any chances.)

Pigs can be stubborn, like people,

which makes them difficult to herd.

Pigs that are well taken care of and well fed rarely need the vet.

A pig's insides are pretty much the same as ours, too.

Heart and lungs and liver and kidneys and stomach— they're all in the same places as ours are, and pigs, like people, can eat meat or vegetables or both.

Like people (or at least people who have been potty-trained), pigs have very clean habits and will never soil their own nests.

Have you noticed how often

I've said that pigs are like people?

That's one of the reasons I like them so much.

There is one big difference, though.

People can be good-looking or
just ordinary-looking or plain ugly.
But all pigs are beautiful.

*There are little
pigs and big pigs, pigs
with long snouts and pigs
with short snouts, pigs with
ears that stick up and pigs
with ears that flop down.
But all pigs are
beautiful.*